My Tena. ₃₃ ʙody

我空出来的身体

Yu Yoyo

余幼幼

My Tenantless Body

我空出来的身体

Translated from Chinese by
A.K. Blakemore and Dave Haysom

poetry
translation
centre

First published in 2019
by the Poetry Translation Centre Ltd
The Albany, Douglas Way, London, SE8 4AG

www.poetrytranslation.org

Some of the Chinese poems printed here first appeared in the journals
Xibu, *Zuojia*, and *Tequ Wenxue*; and in Yu's collection *Me as Bait* (Sichuan
Arts and Literature Publishing House; 2016).

ISBN: 978-0-9575511-3-8

A catalogue record for this book is available from the British Library

Typeset in Minion by Poetry Translation Centre Ltd

Series Editor: Edward Doegar
Cover Design: Kit Humphrey
Printed in the UK by T.J. International

The PTC is supported using public funding by
Arts Council England

Supported using public funding by
**ARTS COUNCIL
ENGLAND**
LOTTERY FUNDED

Contents

Introduction

Yu Yoyo's poetry exists in a place of darkness punctuated by gleams of moonlight and the burning tips of cigarettes. A place where nature is violent: mountains ravenous, sunsets suicidal, waters hostile. Where human presences remain indistinct, sometimes reduced to a role (mother, father, lover) or a selection of disassembled body parts, sometimes summoned as an anonymous addressee, sometimes spliced with trains, ships, and machinery. Sex can never be detached from the umbilical cord, the uterus, the ultrasound room; youth is the fleeting thrill of late nights and hard drinks, but old age can only be put off for so long.

In the world of Chinese literature, authors are generally divided into cohorts bracketed by the decade of their birth, and – because she happened to be born in 1990 – Yu was drafted into the vanguard of the 'nineties generation' by default. Her early works were often treated by critics less as actual poems and more as artefacts of precocity, testaments to the astonishing miracle of a fourteen-year-old girl producing verse – a narrative that she confronted head-on with her choice of pen name: Yòuyòu, meaning youthful or immature.

It was within the online literary communities of the noughties that Yu shaped her unique poetic voice. There she drew inspiration from the forums and message boards where writers shared and dissected each other's work, bypassing the traditional arbiters of literary merit. Though she has now been widely published in journals and magazines, Yu continues to share her writing and paintings directly with readers through her WeChat channel (where she maintains an ongoing sequence of cat-inspired poems that is fast approaching epic-length proportions).

One particular characteristic of Yu's poetry is her sparse use of punctuation. This means that pronouns can appear in the middle of stanzas, without them necessarily revealing whether they are the subject of the action, or the object, or neither. Imperatives coexist with declarative descriptions. A line that appears to have reached end-stopped resolution will yield new interpretations when the subsequent line begins. When working on our translations of these poems, I often found myself thinking about how written poetry changes when it is read aloud, how pausing and intonation can narrow the scope of possible meaning – or reveal alternative interpretations that are imperceptible in the flatness of the page.

The resultant ambiguity is balanced by the specific details that ground Yu's poetry in locations like the Funan River and Zhongshan Street – the geography of her hometown. Far from the coastal metropolises of Beijing, Shanghai and Shenzhen, Sichuan – the southern province best known for its spicy, mouth-numbing cuisine (also: pandas) – has a rich poetic heritage stretching from the Tang dynasty to the 'post-Misty' poets of the nineties like Ouyang Jianghe and Zhai Yongming. In recent years, Sichuan has produced many of the women writers who are currently at the forefront of Chinese literature. Though authors like Yu Yoyo, Yan Ge and Li Jingrui produce very different work – in terms of category (Yan Ge writes fiction, while Li Jingrui specialises in essays and creative nonfiction), content (they all stand at different points on the urban-rural spectrum, for example), and style (such as the extent to which Sichuanese dialect figures in their work) – they share a commitment to stretching the boundaries of their craft.

Most of the poems in this volume are recent works, written after the release of Yu's two collections currently available in Chinese (*Seven Years*, a selection of her output between 2004 and 2011, and *Me As Bait*, published in 2016). The more insistent anaphoric beat that once pulsed through her earlier poems has subsided, while the conversational voice has been destabilised by spikes of syntactic resistance. Yu has spoken of her frustration at prurient critics who interpreted her confessional tone as an invitation to read her work as autobiography, pointing out that women writers have to fight much harder against this fallacy than men. That tone is harder to pinpoint now that the speaker has receded from the foreground of the poems. They retain their visceral intensity, but blend the boundaries of the abstract and the concrete, embodying intangible concepts while paring physical objects down to an immaterial essence. Yu Yoyo's poems are composed of opaque shards that generate their power through juxtaposition, producing slow-burn paradoxes that linger in the memory long after reading.

Dave Haysom

Poems

老了要成为少女

老了要成为少女
用纯洁的眼光去修补
垮掉地过去

腿和腰一个不落地
摆在显眼的位置
插上鲜花
再用舔瓶盖的方式
庆祝岁月的到来

从红酒的味道里
喝出身体的白皙与紧致

它们不想回到往日
在监视中
堆放废弃的爱人和制度

它们留在此刻
此刻在她们旁边

零点钟声响起
她们开着自己去码头停靠

when i grow up i want to be a girl

when i grow up i want to be a girl
fixing the past
with my spotless glance

legs and waist hang
showcased
arranging cut flowers
innocently licking the lid
of new year

the bodies' glow and tautness
in the taste of wine
they do not want to return
to stacking discarded lovers and systems
under supervision

waist-deep
in the moment

midnight strikes
and girls steer themselves

in to port –

晃荡

整条街都抹了致幻剂
街头的烤鱼店还没打烊
钻进鱼肚为
想死的念头码好佐料
身子轻盈像鱼一样
从A面翻到B面
每一筷子都是在为出窍
的灵魂剥离皮肉

现在好了
赤裸裸地晃荡吧
让酒鬼从胸膛穿过
向坠落的同伴吹一口气
脑袋放进车轮反复碾压
用空瓶子盛装幸存的孤立

想死的人没死
继续沿着酒精的路径晃荡
边走边剔骨
到街尾用一枚软月亮
救活杀你的人

sway

the grilled fish place still open
and this entire street seems high

perforate the fish belly
to season the thought of death
lithe slippery body
flipping side A side B
chopsticks peeling the skin
so the soul can be free

it's over now
sway
completely naked
let the drunks puff air
at their staggering friends
put the skull in a wheel
crushed over and over
stopper the isolation
up in a bottle

the people who want to die haven't
but move along in this glazed rut
picking out the bones as they go

toward the soft moon at the end of the street
rekindling
who killed you

爸爸

爸爸
宣判我死亡吧
这样
我空出来的身体
你正好可以住进去
不需要墓穴

不再有孤独症患者
来娶走我
没有另一个女人
恨我

爸爸
你可以把我制作成
床
做我的统治者
妈妈也不认识我
我被压在身下
不认识你们

爸爸
梦快醒了
我要睡觉了
二十一岁就要死了

dad

dad
sentence me to death
so you can live inside my tenantless body
and will not need a tomb

the lonely obsessives
won't come to marry me away
and there will be no *other woman*
hating me

dad
you can make me into bed
be the ruler of me
mum doesn't know me
like i don't know either of you
when i'm held down
under a body

dad
i woke up dreaming
that i went to sleep
that i died at twenty-one

夜游症

1

你出生前的结构
被画在床单上
出生后的性格被
钉在墙壁上
你出生时穿越了
一年中最长的黑夜
只为了
让第二次出生
不那么费劲

你向上寻找乳房
向下寻找脚印

天亮的时候
你长得像你的父亲
天黑的时候
长得像你的母亲

sleepwalking

1

your foetus
tinting the sheets
your adult personality
tacked to the wall

being birthed
from the year's longest darkness
made the second birth
less difficult

you grope upward for the breast
downward for the footprints

under a bright sky
you look like your father

under dark
your mother

2

凌晨三点
你抱着一棵树
因为
没有人抱着你

他们沿着府南河撒尿
一泡接一泡
盖过了
花坛里呕吐物的哭声

有人留下来继续数
透明液体的度数
数到五十二
就有点神志不清

他们借来肝脏与胆汁
借来高兴的理由
还从你那儿借走了
你和生日蛋糕

2

at three o'clock in the morning
you put your arms around a tree
because there's no-one to put their arms
around you

they're noisily pissing in the Funan River
drowning the squeal of vomit
in the flower beds

the remainder
count the proof of their liquor –
a little muddled
by the time they get
to fifty-two

they borrow liver and gall
and a reason to be cheerful

take you away from yourself
take

your birthday cake as well

3

去远一点的地方睡觉
你与摆渡船发生了关系
会不会导致怀孕

她们是夜晚分泌的荷尔蒙
你不太一样
没有人让你平躺
也没有疼痛让你弯腰

你只想坐在一个
很陡很长的土坡上
看楼房与月光
滑进嘉陵江

你一起身
水便漫过头顶

3

on the ride out to sleep
you had relations with the ferry boat

will this result in pregnancy?

the girls all circadian hormone -
but you're not cramping up or impelled
to lie down

you just want to sit
on a steep embankment
watching buildings and moonlight
slip into the Jialing River

when you stand
water spills from
your crown

4

说起之前
居住过的城市
你把伤心表现得很多余

伤心是你用来
造一座桥的材料
你要到对岸去度过晚上
把身体交给
不反光的人

接下来
你可以专注地
对待伤心
在难以承受之时
突然明白
那座城市除了桥
再也没有其他

4

talking about cities
you used to live in
your sorrow seems
superflous

you built a bridge
out of that sorrow
and crossed to give your body
to someone lustreless

afterward
found it easier to pin
the sorrow down

came to an understanding
through the pangs

that aside from the bridge
this city has nothing

5

整个夏天你都在逃跑
逃跑的路线
和脊椎一样垂直
屁股正好落在夜市的中心

中山路的表面
有一层烤焦的酥皮
它同样垂直于某根主干道
七月的某天
牙齿的咬合度
就在这里呈现为一个直角

蜜汁烤排骨、老友粉、冰神甜品……
统统都进入到
没有照明的胃中

你的饱腹感
有时是因为对逃逸的满足
有时是因为灯光的填充

5

spend all summer running straight as backbone
until you find your ass
downtown again

Zhongshan Street
with its straight lines of scorched pastry
on a day in July
mastication's geometry

honey-roast ribs, Laoyou noodles, Bingshen desserts...
all enter
the aphotic belly

your sense of satiety
sometimes derived from the thrill of escape
sometimes from the mallow of lamp-light

6

汽车把你载到
一个叫有陇的地方
国境线在
你的身后吞咽着洪水

你与危险之间
隔着八个太阳和
一小时时差

你要去的地方
云干得比
你离开的地方快

车子继续向南开
天色黯淡
看不见云的地方
你就该停下来

6

you're driven to
a place called Huu Lung
at your back the national border
a gullet of floodwaters

you put
eight suns
and a one-hour time difference
between yourself and danger

you want to go somewhere
the clouds dry faster

driving south
the sky becoming overcast
the place the clouds incorporate
is where you want to stop

7

还剑湖把水下到了天上
你绕着还剑湖走
也想到天上去

天上的水反过来
下到你身上
你湿得只剩下了重力

你哪儿也去不了
穿着这个国家
引以为傲的拖鞋
在屋檐下踱步
难以入眠

你想起更南方的地域
湄公河的水
还不曾
打湿过你的衣角

7

Hoàn Kiem bares its waters up to the sky
walking the banks
you wish you could rise with them

but the waters in the sky
release on your body
until you're so wet you only know gravity

nowhere you can go
in your Ho Chi Minh sandals
they're so proud of here
pacing under the eaves
struggling to sleep

you think of the south
the flowing Mekong River

yet to soak your clothes

8

你有了发动机
高原再也没有了
高原变得
和你一样高
有时候倾斜着
把松林和法国佬的洋房
抖落到脚下

你认识了一个日本人
白昼再也没有了
你坐在他的面前
他做菜给你吃
吃下去的每一口
都像拽着
无边无际的黑暗

你点燃发动机离开
一路都在回想
黑暗真是个美味的东西

8

you still have the engine
but not the plateau –
the plateau grew
as tall as you
and sometimes canted
to scatter at its feet the pine forests
and elegant chalets –

you met a Japanese man
and then daylight was lost to you
sat opposite him
as he prepared food

every bite
like hauling
limitless darkness

you start the engine to go
and spend the whole journey thinking

darkness is truly a delicious thing

9

火车来了
火车下面全是腿疾
它与曲折的路途
形成了脱臼与骨折

火车不停地来
载着
撕碎的银河
倒卖给失眠的人

你睡在铁路边
的小房子
等待失眠的降临

火车一瘸一拐地来了
你用一双好腿
换来一小块星空

9

the train is coming
on its crippled legs
with its torturous route

the train is always coming
merchandising
a shredded Milky Way
to insomniacs

you sleep in a little house
beside the tracks
waiting for your
own condition

and when the train comes
trade a chipper pair of legs
for that little scrap of galaxy

10

你执意要去坐船
拯救梦中溺水的耳朵
你只打捞起来一段
遥远的声音

声音有点驼背
用尽力气说：
床铺好了
饭菜已经上桌
收了几封信件
客厅换了新吊灯

那天正好夏天结束
门开了一条缝
那段声音
一天比一天
直了起来

10

in the dream your ears drowned
you travel by boat to rescue them
but all you scoop from the water is
a distant voice

little hunchback voice
that says with its last strength:

i've made the bed

dinner's on the table

i've received some letters

changed the lightbulb

it was the last day of summer
the door left open a crack
that little hunchback
straightening up
incrementally

11

一觉醒来
窗外的秋天
轮廓还没有显现

显现出来的事物
被内心隐藏

一个你从深夜走回来
一个你从
身体里爬出去

两个你
挤进尘埃会合
不声不响地
掉在了你的睫毛上

11

outside the window
autumn shadows –

not yet –

but there is a presence
hidden in the heart

one you returns from the wild night
one you
crawls out from the body

they meet
nestling in the motes
falling onto your eyelashes
soundlessly

挽留

1

胡子是没有用的
把太阳挑破，流出脓水
白天还是热得发胀
在人群中弹跳
在桥上弹跳
在房间里弹跳
我和你都怕它突然
弹跳到床上
打开我们的私处

然而，并没有打开什么
它只是站着
离你很近

我帮你修剪了
胡子上的汗珠
整整齐齐的汗珠
亮晶晶的汗珠
一颗一颗全部都
弹回了天上

stay

1

your beard is expendable
pop the sun and let the pus drip out
hot enough by day to cause swelling

it bounces through the crowds
bounces on the bridge
bounces in the room
we are afraid
it might bounce onto the bed
and open up our legs

but it hasn't opened anything yet
it just stands there
close to you

i'm giving you a trim
and the beads of sweat on your stubble
so neatly strung
so sparkling

they bounce into the sky
one by one

2

我冷冷的
不止一次劝你
从飞机上跳下来
像皮球一样
像白天的温度一样
跳下来
不要那么慌张
不要带着欺骗
跳下来
四肢张开
像做爱那样
你在上
大地在下

我冷冷的
以为你会跳下来

2

i ask
coldly
and repeatedly
that you jump from the plane
like a rubber ball
like the temperature
of day

jump now
just relax
stop lying

spread your limbs
like you're making love
you on top
the earth underneath

coldly
i thought you could jump down

3

实际上你已经
在我的身边
我们是两个没有意义的人
想起来你做的
水煮肉片很好吃
我做的番茄炒蛋很难吃
由此抵消了一些
不切实际

之后呢
你加上盐，我减去糖
你乘以面粉，我除以大米
也将不存在意义

3

in actuality
we are already joined –
two pointless people

you boiled beef slices and they tasted good
my fried eggs and tomato
terrible

a balance
unrealistic

you added salt
i took away the sugar
i divided the rice and
you multiplied by flour

meaningless signifiers

4

我希望的是
一切并没有那么不堪
可以不关灯
可以不裸体
我可以不知道
你的手除了
抚摸拉萨河水
还抚摸过无数女人的身体
你的眼睛除了
包容阿克苏的干裂
还包容了一位
女孩的潮湿

你也可以不知道
我最深处的心已死
只留一件
轻薄的衣裳
在你怀中飘来飘去

4

my hope
that things will not be so unbearable
it will be possible to keep the light on
it will be possible to remain clothed

i will un-know
how you touched your hand
to the bodies of other women
and the swelling waters
of the Lhasa

that in your eyes
the badlands of the Aksu
were moistened
by girl

and you will un-know the dark heart in
the deepest part of me –
just the light clothes

floating in your arms

5

你说你做梦了
梦见在越南嫖妓
不知道是河内
还是西贡
可能是大叻
可能在
地图上根本找不到

现在只有与
星星接壤的地方
能让我坦诚：
我没有去过越南
也不打算原谅你的梦

5

you said you were dreaming
dreamed that you were cruising for girls
in Vietnam –

don't know if it was Hanoi
or Saigon
maybe Dalat
maybe somewhere
you can't find on a map

now star-fringed lands
make me candid –

i have never been to
Vietnam

nor do i intend
to forgive this dream

6

你四处买船
准备从一座城市
漂到与它不相邻的
另外一座城市

你想要的船
船身与河水粘连着
强行撕开
几乎无法治愈
伤口的创面

此后
如果没有被浪掀翻
也会被情绪掀翻

你和我
被搓成拴在船舷上
的一根麻绳
注定要在
宽阔的河面
拉起两条人命

6

you rent a boat
prepare to drift from one city
to a further city

this boat of yours
its hull adheres to the water
force them apart and find
a sucking wound

if a wave doesn't capsize you
turbulence will

a rope
twisted round the boat's side
destines us to pull from the bed

two drenched human lives

7

想起自己很可笑
就着荤段子下酒
也能三五下把自个撂翻

我其实很难过
比倒空的酒瓶还要
找不到重心

从白天走过的铁轨上
摇摇晃晃
再走进废弃的意识里
我有一个
生了霉的月亮
还有一些拐了弯
就消失不见的挽留

7

i find myself funny
dirty joke with chaser
knocks me upside down in
seconds

and i feel bad actually
centre of gravity off
like an empty bottle

wavering out of daylight
down railroad tracks
into castoff consciousness

i have
this mouldering moon
and will soon lose sight
of these pleadings
to stay

空城

把孤独扛在肩上
肚脐以上的部位都视为无效
比如去喝一杯水
应该打破它的实际意义
不是人体需求
而是要把空荡的房间
全部淹没

来去的声音都把
你当作码头一样环绕
接着是电视机里的人像
正在施行暴力
而你却毫发无伤
这未免太过无趣

过节的人也都与你形同陌路
不在此地停留的意义
或许是身体的直接命令

城里的人越来越少
逐渐要被一片汪洋取代

empty town

carry loneliness on your shoulder
from the navel upward void

collapse
the physiological necessity
of drinking a glass of water –
this the total inundation
of your torso's empty chamber

you're like a pier
wrapped in sounds
of arrival and departure

the people on TV
violating one another
while you remain just intact
and a little bored

the debauchees don't stop here
retrocede under bodily impulse

fewer and fewer people in the city
gradually replaced

by an expanse of water

Afterword

A.K. Blakemore, one of the co-translators of this selection of Yu Yoyo's poetry, writes in an essay for *Poetry Foundation*:

> Sometimes I come home from work after dark and strip lights in my kitchen will not turn on straight away, but instead flash abortively, and I stand in the hallway turning the switch on and off as my black cat walks across the linoleum floor, and is visible only in these flashes, a few strides further at each gasp of the light that will not work. And I think, that is how we should move from one thing to another in a poem.

This could easily be a description of the lithe, darting brilliance of Yu's own poetry – language which does not waste time bedding itself in, or explaining itself to you; but which simply jumps from arresting idea to arresting idea with electrifying intent. It is in this caustic, sharp movement that Yu forms her poetics, one which is crucially and importantly a poetics of youth. Yu, born in 1990, (thoroughly a 'millennial'), has created a poetic language which has seemingly never not known the internet – its caustic, flat wit; its complete lack of punctuation; its blunt delivery and its incredible linguistic speed. Mandarin itself has no tenses, and, (even in a translation that must force tenses back into the work), Yu's use of this flexibility to create temporally ambiguous language is felt – rendering the eternal now created by the web, where the wounds of the past, present and future flicker and blink simultaneously, as if freshly made.

Though internet culture varies substantially across nations – especially as certain websites easily available in the UK are not available in mainland China – it is still fair to say that the constantly updating responses of WeChat, WhatsApp, Weibo, email, twitter and beyond, share a totalising verbal immediacy. The language of the internet jumps from meme, to in-joke, to group chat, Instagram caption and back again, leaving no time for formal investment or longeurs. Yu has taken this febrile, energetic, jagged diction, and has brought it into poetry.

Yu is a poet of youth not only in her appropriation of the urgent, fluid diction of the internet, but within the very meat and blood of her poetic concerns. Yu's subject itself, in these poems, seems to be the tremors of a self shuddering between youth and adulthood. Yu captures, with electric precision, the strange transitions that take place when a person is, in the immortal words of Britney Spears 'not a girl, not yet a woman.' Yu paints in the cloudy strangeness of the time between teenagerhood and one's late twenties – feeling sometimes too childish to make any choices about anything, and sometimes too ancient, too long bruised and heartbroken to even get up in the mornings. Yu's poems offer us the ravenous potential of this unstable time. They show us the pain of the self stretching and becoming itself; of disappointing relationships which don't offer the transcendent knowledge one might hope for; the threat and expectation of the youthful female body; the fear of living within a time of cultural extremity and environmental collapse.

To suggest that Yu's poems are 'universal' in these explorations of becoming would be naive, and would undermine the specificity of their experience of place. Yu's poems reflect growing up in a quickly changing global mega-power. City dwellers in China often live lives unrecognisable to their parents, and certainly their grandparents – a hyper quick transition of economic, political and cultural experience which creates a particularly intense version of youth's singularity and generational separation. The poems also reflect Yu's specific home landscape; its rivers and mountains, its busy streets and its humid summers. Yet, as a British reader I still find something relatable in the bright, electric energy of their youthful exploration, the city and towns they run through seemingly flimsy backdrops to the adventures and terrors of being alive, of coming into one's body. Desiring to be comforted and escape all at the same time – to fill the mysterious and hidden places of the developing self, where we are unknown to even ourselves.

The poems, in this deft, dagger sharp translation, aren't obviously 'thematic,' they don't tell neatly packaged, commoditised poetic stories – rather they follow the minute permutations of a self's experience. Many of the contemporary movements in contemporary Chinese poetry can be seen as different reactions to the profoundly influential 1980's Menglong (misty/obscure) tradition, whose poetry was extremely subjective and symbolic. Contemporary poets such as Yi Sha and Han Dong work to make poetry more transparent and colloquial; and poets such as Zang Di use language games and 'academic' linguistic deconstruction to challenge subjectivity and lyricism. Yu's work cuts a path that does not fit neatly into either of these more 'academic' or 'colloquial' traditions, creating a language that is paradoxically mysterious and direct. Yu's poetry is one that charts the fluctuations of emotion and thought, never obscure, but also never treating language as a system able to contain and hold down a permanence of meaning. Simultaneously lyric and philosophically challenging, Yu has crafted a poetic voice able to record the transformations of a being in flux.

Indeed, Yu's work puts me in mind of the experimental fiction of Claire-Louise Bennett in *Pond*, fragile accounts of experience without a contracting 'plot' – translations of inner feeling, made visible in the strange spaces of language. Like Bennett, Yu traces the ways in which our consciousness responds to, and is created by, the surrounding world meeting the individual body:

one you returns from the wild night
one you
crawls out from the body

they meet
nestling in the motes
falling onto your eyelashes
soundlessly   ('sleepwalking')

The 'wild night' meets and creates the selves responding to it. This self, the youthful, expanding self made up of many kaleidoscopic versions of itself, is a permeable membrane. Not something fixed, but something permanently in flux. Yu is able to chart this liminal form of becoming, bring it into poetic language.

Despite the pleasurable excitement and excess of youth that Yu shows us, these poems are also laced with the insecurity and fear of growing up on a planet which may not outlast you; and the societal fissures that flow from that. In Yu's poetic world, nature is necessary and liberating, but it is not the beautiful, timeless vision we see in classical Chinese poetry. Nature offers potential freedom, at the same time that it is full of latent, utterly modern threat and suffering.

In the first poem of the 'stay' sequence she writes, 'pop the sun and let the pus drip out / hot enough by day to cause swelling.' The sun becomes a wound, pouring its effluent onto the earth beneath it. This sense of the nonhuman world as danger is also emphasised in 'empty town':

the people on TV
violating one another
while you remain just intact
and a little bored
the debauchees don't stop here
retrocede under bodily impulse

> fewer and fewer people in the city
> gradually replaced
>
> by an expanse of water

Here Yu gives us the voice of a youth 'a little bored' by the violence and destruction they witness expanding around them. But her voice does not satirise or critique this youthful numbness and cynicism – rather, in this poem, such coldness seems the only bearable response to a society saturated in violence; a home being slowly drained of its citizens, replaced by flood. In these poems we dive into what it feels like living within the constant, painful tension of a crisis you didn't create – daily experience inevitably tied up with the fear of global strife and destruction. These nuanced poems give words to the strange reality of the global 'millennial' – working to create a future which may crumble under their feet.

These poems also pay particular attention to another multifaceted, and potentially painful element of youth's experience – gender. They explore what youth might feel like within a female body, and the complications that living within such a body can bring. They turn the hot, messy concern of womanhood into a subject suitable for poetic exploration and, in doing so, fracture what we expect from the form. As A.K. Blakemore says in her *Poetry Foundation* essay, 'If you are a woman, writing about your experience of being a woman, you are part of one of the most avant-garde literary movements there has ever been'. Yu gives us this necessary, avant-garde experience of femaleness and the pressure a female body can create. In poem 3 of the 'sleepwalking' sequence she writes:

> on the ride out to sleep
> you had relations with the ferry boat
>
> will this result in pregnancy?

the girls all circadian hormone –
but you're not cramping up or impelled
to lie down

you just want to sit
on a steep embankment
watching buildings and moonlight
slip into the Jialing River

The surreal comedy of 'you had relations with the ferry boat/ will this result in pregnancy' reminds us of stories in school playgrounds of getting knocked up from sitting on toilet seats. Every surface is latent, leering with fertile potential – the female body an inevitability, a blank canvas that must be, will be filled. Yu links up this potentiality with the girls interconnected hormones, a hot circle of bodies and signals where biology seems to equal destiny. The pressure of this contained, already laid out way of being is subtly played through the idea of 'cramping;' with the narrator rejecting the cramped, predictable forms her body might be encouraged to be in. All she wants is to watch 'buildings and moonlight/ slip into the Jialing River,' to see structures, limits, melt and pour away. This desire for flux and undoing circles out from the narrator, wishing her away from, beyond, the gender that seeks to control her.

In poem 10 of the 'sleepwalking' sequence Yu moves from the pressures on hormonal girls, to imagining the, perhaps equally constrained, life of an adult woman. Here, a 'little hunchback voice' lists 'with the last of its strength' a variety of tasks: 'i've made the bed / dinner's on the table / i've received some letters / changed the lightbulb', and the poem concludes:

it was the last day of summer
the door left open a crack
that little hunchback

straightening up
incrementally

Again, in this poem, Yu uses her direct, flat diction to parse out the subtleties of a particularly female difficulty. A quiet, simplistic 'little hunchback voice' offers up statements to what we must imagine as a male figure, listing the tasks it has completed – domesticity as offering, as value. This voice is weak, bent over, pressed down by the blandness of its daily life, of the banality it must live and utter. The voice gives us no specificity – this could be any woman, almost anywhere in the world, tired out from drudgery and emotional labour.

It is only when the door opens to show a sliver of summer, that we have the strange image of a voice 'straightening up / incrementally' – a voice that, much like in the third poem of the sequence, again finds freedom in the openness of the nonhuman world, of light that can flow and go anywhere. The 'voice' straightens, and we must think that the voice of the poem straightens too, language escaping a gendered obedience through a vision of incorporeality, slipping out of cliché, and into the vibrating possibilities of poetic expression. The body is imagined here as a limit, and poetic language as a way to move from its confines, a form of transcendent evasion.

This, then, is a deeply feminist poem, that enacts its feminism without a moment of didacticism or overt politics – rather it listens to the tenor of restraint in a woman's domestic voice, and puts in on the page. There is no fuss, no bells or whistles, in this form of writing; only an exact practice of attention to where minds, where bodies, might be forced to bend and prostrate themselves. The poetry attends to such degradation as if, by putting it into language, there might be a way to confront it, comprehend it, and most crucially – escape it.

Rebecca Tamás

Born in Sichuan in 1990, Yu Yoyo started publishing poetry at the age of fourteen. Her work has featured in various literary journals and anthologies, and she has published two collections, *Seven Years* (Sichuan Arts and Literature Publishing House; 2012) and *Me as Bait* (Sichuan Arts and Literature Publishing House; 2016). Her poems have been translated into several languages, including English, Korean, Russian, French, Japanese, and Swedish, and within China she has received numerous literary prizes. In 2017 she was a fellow of the Vermont Studio Center / Henry Luce Translation Program.

A K Blakemore is the author of two full-length collections of poetry: *Humbert Summer* (Eyewear, 2015) and *Fondue* (Offord Road Books, 2018). *Fondue* was shortlisted for the 2019 Ledbury Forte Prize for Best Second Collection. Her work has been widely published and anthologised, appearing in publications including *Poetry*, *The London Review of Books* and *The Poetry Review*. She lives in London.

Dave Haysom has been translating, editing, and writing about contemporary Chinese literature since 2012. He was the joint managing editor of *Pathlight* magazine from 2014 to 2018, and has recently translated novels by Feng Tang, Li Er, and Xu Zechen. His portfolio is online at spittingdog.net.

Rebecca Tamás works as a Lecturer in Creative Writing at York St John University. She is the editor, with Sarah Shin, of *Spells: Occult Poetry for the 21st Century* (Ignota Books, 2018). Her first collection of poetry, *WITCH* (Penned in the Margins, 2019), is a Poetry Book Society Spring Recommendation and a *Paris Review* Staff Pick.

About the Poetry Translation Centre

Set up in 2004, the Poetry Translation Centre is the only UK organisation dedicated to translating, publishing and promoting contemporary poetry from Africa, Asia and Latin America. We introduce extraordinary poets from around the world to new audiences through books, online resources and bilingual events. We champion diversity and representation in the arts, and forge enduring relations with diaspora communities in the UK. We explore the craft of translation through our long-running programme of workshops which are open to all.

The Poetry Translation Centre is based in London and is an Arts Council National Portfolio organisation. To find out more about us, including how you can support our work, please visit: www.poetrytranslation.org.

About the World Poet Series

The *World Poet Series* offers an introduction to some of the world's most exciting contemporary poets in an elegant pocket-sized format. The books are presented as bilingual editions, with the English and original-language text displayed side by side. The translations themselves have emerged from specially commissioned collaborations between leading English-language poets and bridge-translators. Completing each book is an afterword essay by a UK-based poet, responding to the translations.